DECISION TIME MARRIAGE SERIES:

Dealing with Conflicts and Anger in Marriage

Paapa Owusu-Manu

Published by New Generation Publishing in 2018

Copyright © Paapa Owusu-Manu 2018

First Edition

The author asserts the moral right under the Copyright, Designs and Patents Act 1988 to be identified as the author of this work.

All Rights reserved. No part of this publication may be reproduced, stored in a retrieval system or transmitted, in any form or by any means without the prior consent of the author, nor be otherwise circulated in any form of binding or cover other than that in which it is published and without a similar condition being imposed on the subsequent purchaser.

www.newgeneration-publishing.com

New Generation Publishing

Table of Contents

EFFECTIVE COMMUNICATION 1
- *DECISION TIME- MAKE EVERY EFFORT TO DEFUSE ANGER AND TENSION.* 2

DEALING WITH MARITAL CONFLICTS, MOCKING AND DISTRESS 3
- *DECISION TIME: PRAY FOR YOUR HUSBAND/WIFE ALWAYS AND FORGIVE EACH OTHER IN THE MIGHTY NAME OF JESUS CHRIST* 4

UPROOTING AND OVERTHROWING POOR COMMUNICATION & MARITAL CONFLICTS 5
- *DECISION TIME- DEMONSTRATE LOVE, RESPECT AND KINDNESS IN YOUR MARRIAGE* 6
- **WISDOM FOR PEACEFUL MARRIAGE** 7
- *DECISION TIME. TURN YOUR HUSBAND/ WIFE'S MISTAKE INTO NEW STYLES.* 8

PRAYER FOR MARRIAGES 9

IT IS YOUR RESPONSIBILITY TO HELP YOUR HUSBAND/ WIFE TO OVERCOME THEIR WEAKNESSES 10

UPROOT ANGER IN MARRIAGE 10
- *DECISION TIME: REFUSE TO ALLOW ANGER TO LABEL YOU AS A FOOL* 12

MY PRAYER POEM FOR PEACEFUL MARRIAGE 13
- *DECISION TIME: GET RID OF SELFISHNESS, BITTERNESS, UNFORGIVENESS, ANGER AND LIES IN MARRIAGE* 15

DEALING WITH ANGER IN MARRIAGE 1 16
- *DECISION TIME: FIGHT AND OVERCOME ANGER WITH LOVE AND PRAYERS* 16

DEALING WITH ANGER IN MARRIAGE 2 17
  *DECISION TIME: RESIST THE DEVIL WITH
  YOUR FORGIVENESS AND LOVE 19*

DEALING WITH MARITAL CONFLICTS: WHOSE FAULTS? 20
  *DECISION TIME: LOVE YOUR SPOUSE JUST AS
  S/HE IS 22*

CONGRATULATIONS - AVOID UNNECESSARY DELAYS. 23

Quotes

> Overcome marital conflicts by genuine and sincere love.
> - Paapa Owusu-Manu

EFFECTIVE COMMUNICATION

Let your communication and speech be seasoned with anger and conflict defusers.

Be patient in your speech by giving soft or gentle responses.

Make conscious effort to communicate with your partner. You need to spend some time with your spouse. Give him/her the attention he/she deserves. If you do not give your partner attention to communicate with you. He/she will find someone somehow to engage in communication.

Lack of communication in marriage is one of the major sources of most marital conflicts. Bear in mind that your spouse will not know all your good intentions about him/her unless you communicate. Your partner cannot conjure the meaning for your actions and reactions.

If you do not speak out, he/she may misinterpret your actions for you and the consequences will not be pleasant.

A gentle answer turns away wrath, but a harsh word stirs up anger. A hot-tempered person stirs up conflict, but the one who is patient calms a quarrel. - Proverbs 15:1,18

DECISION TIME: MAKE EVERY EFFORT TO DEFUSE ANGER AND TENSION.

> Let your communication and speech be seasoned with anger and conflict defusers.
> Paapa Owusu-Manu

DEALING WITH MARITAL CONFLICTS, MOCKING AND DISTRESS

In the mighty name of Jesus Christ:

Every attack, mocking and distress in your marriage be ceased.

Terminate every form of marital conflicts.

Any external forces and influences disturbing your marriage be uprooted and broken.

1. God should put confusion between your husband/wife and the external forces/influences.
2. May God silence your enemies and mockers in your marriage.
3. May your husband/wife listen to you and ignore your adversaries.
4. May the peace of God fill your marriage and household.
5. May your husband/wife love you alone.
6. May your husband/wife respect and honour you.
7. May your husband/wife show you kindness and cherish you always.
8. May the Holy Spirit take over your marriage and guide you in every aspect of your marriage and household.
9. May the fear of God be in your marriage at all times. AMEN!!!.

But Sarah saw that the son whom Hagar the Egyptian had borne to Abraham was mocking, and she said to Abraham, "Get rid of that slave woman and her son, for that woman's son will never share in the inheritance with my son Isaac." The matter distressed Abraham greatly because it concerned his son. But God said to him, "Do not be so distressed about the boy and your slave woman. Listen to whatever Sarah tells you, because it is through Isaac that your offspring will be reckoned. I will make the son of the slave into a nation also, because he is your offspring." - Genesis 21:9-13

> Your partner cannot conjure the meaning for your actions and reactions. If you do not speak out, he/she may misinterpret your actions for you and the consequences will not be pleasant.
> -Paapa Owusu-Manu

DECISION TIME: PRAY FOR YOUR HUSBAND/WIFE ALWAYS AND FORGIVE EACH OTHER IN THE MIGHTY NAME OF JESUS CHRIST

UPROOTING AND OVERTHROWING POOR COMMUNICATION & MARITAL CONFLICTS

In the mighty name of Jesus Christ:

1. Father, I thank you for peace in my marriage.
2. Father, I thank you that you have given my husband/wife a loving and kind heart towards me.
3. Lord, I thank you that the communication in our marriage is enhanced by the power of the Holy Spirit.
4. Father, I thank you that you have caused my husband/wife to understand and be considerate to me.
5. Father, I thank you that you have caused my husband/wife to remember his/her first love.
6. Lord, I thank you that your Spirit has taken control of our marriage.
7. Father, I thank you that you have caused my husband/wife and I to forgive each other.
8. May the Lord rebuke every demon/ witchcraft frustrating our marriage in the mighty name of Jesus Christ.
9. May the Lord rebuke every agent fighting the peace in our marriage.
10. I command every opposition and external influences in my marriage to die by fire.

11. Father, I thank you that you have uprooted and destroyed any spirit of greed, selfishness and jealousy in my marriage in the mighty name of Jesus Christ.
12. Father, I thank you that you have completely removed every hatred, pride and disrespect from my marriage in the mighty name of Jesus Christ.

A gentle answer turns away wrath, but a harsh word stirs up anger. The soothing tongue is a tree of life, but a perverse tongue crushes the spirit. Better a little with the fear of the Lord than great wealth with turmoil. Better a small serving of vegetables with love than a fattened calf with hatred. A hot-tempered person stirs up conflict, but the one who is patient calms a quarrel. - Proverbs 15:1,4,16-18

DECISION TIME- DEMONSTRATE LOVE, RESPECT AND KINDNESS IN YOUR MARRIAGE

> It is your responsibility to help your husband/wife to overcome his/her weaknesses.
> - Paapa Owusu-Manu

WISDOM FOR PEACEFUL MARRIAGE

REMEMBER:

1. Patience increases love in marriage.
2. Anger destroys peace in marriage.
3. Kindness and sharing promote love, peace and happiness in marriage.
4. Envy, selfishness and greed destroy the sweetness in marriage.
5. Lording it over your partner (husband or wife) breeds conflicts and divisions in marriage.
6. Submission and mutual respect demonstrate maturity in marriage.
7. Pride creates dents in marriage (you are not better than your wife or husband. You are co- heirs in the grace of God).
8. Me, myself and I bring marital conflicts. Replace (me, myself and I with we, us and ours).
9. Honour and respect your husband/ wife as often as you can and never dishonour him/ her particularly in public.
10. Forgive the wrongs, weaknesses, failures and shortcomings of your husband/ wife. Cover and shield your partner's faults.
11. Destroy and completely delete your book/file of recording your wife/husband's mistakes with dates.

12. Develop trust and hope in your husband/ wife. Protect him/her all the time and persevere to change his/her shortfalls into new styles.

Love is patient, love is kind. It does not envy, it does not boast, it is not proud. It does not dishonour others, it is not self-seeking, it is not easily angered, it keeps no record of wrongs. Love does not delight in evil but rejoices with the truth. It always protects, always trusts, always hopes, always perseveres. Love never fails. But where there are prophecies, they will cease; where there are tongues, they will be stilled; where there is knowledge, it will pass away.
- 1 Corinthians 13:4-8

1 Peter 3:7 (AMP)
⁷ In the same way, you husbands, live with your wives in an understanding way [with great gentleness and tact, and with an intelligent regard for the marriage relationship], as with someone physically weaker, since she is a woman. Show her honour and respect as a fellow heir of the grace of life, so that your prayers will not be hindered or ineffective.

DECISION TIME. TURN YOUR HUSBAND/ WIFE'S MISTAKE INTO NEW STYLES.

> My smiles and laughter ignite smiles and laughter from my spouse to trigger good communication, love and affections.
> - Paapa Owusu-Manu

PRAYER FOR MARRIAGES

Happy and Peaceful Marriage

IT IS YOUR RESPONSIBILITY TO HELP YOUR HUSBAND/ WIFE TO OVERCOME THEIR WEAKNESSES

Understand and accept that everybody has some weaknesses as well as strengths.

Do not dwell too much on the weaknesses of your spouse, but rather appreciate him or her on their strengths.

Make every effort to help your spouse to deal with his/her weaknesses with encouragement, patience, love, kindness and prayers.

Uproot Anger in Marriage

Anger can make someone a slave without the person realising that s/he is a slave.

Anger creates so many problems for people in all aspects of life.

Anger destroys peace and steals the joy in many marriages

Anger brings divorce and separation in marriages.

Anger is the highway of many marital conflicts.

Remember: Refuse to be labelled as a fool.

PRAYER:

In the mighty name of Jesus Christ:
1. Father, help me to overcome every anger in my life.

2. Father, help my husband/ wife to overcome anger related issues.
3. I bind every spirit of anger affecting my marriage.
4. I root out every anger from my husband/ wife's life.
5. I refuse to be labelled as a fool because of anger.
6. My husband/wife can never be a fool because of outbursts of anger.
7. My husband/wife and I will not entertain anger any longer in our marriage.
8. I love my husband/wife . Therefore, you spirit of anger you have lost the battle.
9. I respect my husband/wife and cherish my marriage.
10. We cast out anger from our marriage and we will not allow it to ruin our peace and what the Lord has joined together.
11. When my husband/wife becomes angry, I refuse to react to his/her anger.
12. The Holy Spirit is in charge of our marriage. Therefore, anger back off in the mighty name of Jesus Christ. AMEN!!!

Do not be quickly provoked in your spirit, for anger resides in the lap of fools. - Ecclesiastes 7:9 NIV

Don't become angry quickly, because anger is foolish. - Ecclesiastes 7:9 ERV

Control your temper, for anger labels you a fool. - Ecclesiastes 7:9 NLT

DECISION TIME: REFUSE TO ALLOW ANGER TO LABEL YOU AS A FOOL

> If you are able to change your ways and renew your mind, your crooked spouse will gradually fit into your style.
> - Paapa Owusu-Manu

MY PRAYER POEM FOR PEACEFUL MARRIAGE

I have learned from experience and school of marriage the following:

1. The more I love my wife/husband, the better her/his behaviour and positive attitude towards me.
2. Anytime I pray for him/her, the greater peace and happiness we both enjoy.
3. The more good intentions I have for her/him, the greater the love and bond between us.
4. The moment I despise her/him in my heart, the sooner quarrels, unnecessary arguments and disputes start from nowhere.
5. Anytime, I hold grudges and bitterness in my heart about my wife/ husband, I start to find fault about everything s/he does.
6. The more I keep finding faults, the more over sensitive I become over pettiness and trivialities.
7. The moment I begin to appreciate the good things my husband/wife does, the stronger my love grows.
8. The more my love grows, the deeper the peace I enjoy.
9. The more I speak evil about my spouse, the sooner the thoughts manifest in his/her life and the bitter the troubles I endure.

PRAYER

Father in the mighty name of Jesus Christ:

A. Help me to enjoy my marriage by having happiness and peace with my spouse.

B. Dear Lord Jesus Christ, help me to forgive my spouse for everything s/he has done against me knowingly or unknowingly.

C. Father, help me to love, understand and accept my spouse all the days of my life.

D. Blessed Holy Spirit, assist me to appreciate every little efforts and kindness my spouse does to make our marriage to work. AMEN

But now is the time to get rid of anger, rage, malicious behaviour, slander, and dirty language. Don't lie to each other, for you have stripped off your old sinful nature and all its wicked deeds. Put on your new nature, and be renewed as you learn to know your Creator and become like him. - Colossians 3:8-10 NLT

And "don't sin by letting anger control you." Don't let the sun go down while you are still angry, for anger gives a foothold to the devil. - Ephesians 4:26-27 NLT

DECISION TIME: GET RID OF SELFISHNESS, BITTERNESS, UNFORGIVENESS, ANGER AND LIES IN MARRIAGE

> Lack of communication in marriage is one of the major sources of most marital conflicts.
> - Paapa Owusu-Manu

DEALING WITH ANGER IN MARRIAGE 1

I learned from experience and school of marriage that my happiness in marriage depends on me.

As soon as I become angry, I become prayerless and unlovable.

I have to make myself happy for it is infectious to my spouse.

My smiles and laughter ignite smiles and laughter from my spouse to trigger good communication, love and affections.

I have made a decision to make myself happy always.

I try not to be a victim of anger because it can steal and spoil my happiness in marriage.

And "don't sin by letting anger control you." Don't let the sun go down while you are still angry, for anger gives a foothold to the devil. - Ephesians 4:26-27 NLT

DECISION TIME: FIGHT AND OVERCOME ANGER WITH LOVE AND PRAYERS

> Home is home if I am on good terms with my spouse
> -Paapa Owusu-Manu

DEALING WITH ANGER IN MARRIAGE 2

1. I have learnt by experience in the journey and school of marriage that:
2. I cannot pray when I am angry with my spouse.
3. I worry myself for no reason if I get upset with my partner's shortcomings.
4. I become uneasy if there is no peace at home. My focus, concentration and prayer life get destabilised.
5. I can confidently say that home is home if I am on good terms with my spouse.
6. Home becomes just a house furnished with stuff if there is no peace at home and things turn into pieces.

PRAYER

In the mighty name of Jesus Christ:

1. Father, I thank you that you have delivered me from the spirit of anger.
2. I declare that anger cannot control me again in my life to make mistakes and regret later.
3. I break the power of anger and unforgiveness from my life.
4. I break and uproot the power of anger, unforgiveness and bitterness from my spouse.
5. Lord, for your name's sake, I have forgiven every wrong my spouse has done against me.
6. Father, I will not disobey you by allowing anger to control me to hold bitterness and grudges.
7. Father, I thank you for giving me the grace to deal with any form of anger and bitterness in my marriage.
8. I will not let the sun to go down while I am still angry to give the devil an opportunity to create confusion in my marriage.
9. Devil, I know your schemes, I will not give you a foothold in my marriage because of prolonged anger.
10. I know my spouse has some weaknesses, I have forgiven him/her of all the wrongs.

11. I have made a decision to pray for my spouse to overcome his/her weaknesses instead of holding on to bitterness and resentments.
12. Father, I thank you that you have healed my heart from all wounds of marital conflicts.
13. God the Father, God the Son and Blessed Holy Spirit, I thank you that you have forgiven me all my sins against you and people.

And "don't sin by letting anger control you." Don't let the sun go down while you are still angry, for anger gives a foothold to the devil. - Ephesians 4:26-27 NLT

DECISION TIME: RESIST THE DEVIL WITH YOUR FORGIVENESS AND LOVE

> Home becomes just a house furnished with stuff if there is no peace at home and things turn into pieces
> - Paapa Owusu-Manu

DEALING WITH MARITAL CONFLICTS: WHOSE FAULTS?

Below are some 'wisdom to go' from experience and lessons from the journey and school of Marriage:

After decades of practical experiences, observations and lessons from the Faculty of Marital School; below are some findings:

1. I found that I worried myself and subjected myself to unnecessary stress because I wanted to change what the Lord has made crooked.
2. I tried hard to make straight what the Lord has bent.
3. Men will forever be men and women will forever be women.
4. There are things about men that can never be changed.
5. There are some things about women that can never be changed.
6. Therefore, you change your mind and adapt to your spouse.
7. Try to dance according to the rhythm of your spouse and give yourself some peace.
8. If you are able to change your ways and renew your mind, your crooked spouse will gradually fit into your style.

PRAYER

Father, in the mighty name of Jesus Christ:
1. Grant me peace and happiness in marriage.
2. Give me understanding and wisdom to enjoy my marriage.
3. Father, help me to love my spouse genuinely without any hypocrisy.
4. Give both my husband/wife and I understanding, peace, love, happiness and prosperity in our marriage.
5. Help us to appreciate and accept each other just as we are and the grace to enjoy our marriage.

Don't attempt to change your husband/wife but try to amend your ways and adapt to your husband/wife. Your understanding, consideration, kindness, actions, reaction and love towards your spouse will eventually cause your partner to suit what you desire.

Consider the work of God: Who can make straight what He has bent? - Ecclesiastes 7:13 AMP

Accept the way God does things, for who can straighten what he has made crooked? - Ecclesiastes 7:13 NLT

DECISION TIME: LOVE YOUR SPOUSE JUST AS S/HE IS

> Don't attempt to change your husband/wife but try to amend your ways and adapt to your husband/wife.
> - Paapa Owusu-Manu

CONGRATULATIONS - AVOID UNNECESSARY DELAYS.

May the grace of our Lord Jesus Christ , the Love of God and the sweet fellowship of the Holy Spirit be with you always in your marriage. May the protection of God be your portion today and forevermore.

I pray that your marriage will be peaceful and successful in the mighty name of Jesus Christ.

Avoid unnecessary delays in your marriage when the right person comes.

Don't miss your marital appointment for unnecessary delays and unwarrantable selection criteria.

Don't allow anybody to delay your marriage when God's appointed time for you flags up.

You can only know the appointed moment through prayers and waiting upon the Lord.

The scriptures below shows you how Rebekah narrowly missed her glorious marriage by unjustifiable delays from the family.

Do not allow your selection criteria to bring delay to your marriage. Undue delays may also lead some people to pre-marital sex and sexual immorality.

So tell me—will you or won't you show unfailing love and faithfulness to my master? Please tell me yes or no, and then I'll know what to do next." Then Laban and Bethuel replied, "The Lord has obviously brought you here, so there is nothing we can say.

Here is Rebekah; take her and go. Yes, let her be the wife of your master's son, as the Lord has directed." But he said, "Don't delay me. The Lord has made my mission successful; now send me back so I can return to my master."

So they called Rebekah.

"Are you willing to go with this man?" they asked her. And she replied, "Yes, I will go." - Genesis 24:49-51,56,58 NLT

DECISION TIME: LOVE COVERS MULTITUDES OF SIN

> As soon as I become angry, I become prayerless and unlovable.
> - Paapa Owusu-Manu

ABOUT THE BOOK

Decision Time Marriage Nuggets are prayers and study devotional series to help people, (individuals, marriage couples, families and groups) to enhance their marital life by making every efforts to make their marriages to work. Each daily devotion is comprised of introductory memorable statements, prayers and scriptures to help believers to equip themselves with insights, wisdom, knowledge, spiritual food and nourishment to promote peace in marriages.

Every statement in these "how to make your marriage work nuggets" must be read and applied. Both parties can read and discuss together when necessary.

ABOUT THE AUTHOR

Paapa Owusu-Manu is an ordained minister of God with a dynamic gift of wisdom and diplomacy for the ministry of Jesus Christ.

He has been a qualified teacher for over twenty three years in both Ghana and abroad (London, United Kingdom). His areas of specialties are Business Enterprise and Entrepreneurship Education, Primary and Adult Numeracy, Internal Verification and Quality Assurance, Teacher Training and Inspection Strategies. He has worked and provided consultancy services to over ten HM Prisons/Young Offender Institutes as an OLASS Advanced Practitioner for quality improvement, coaching, and mentoring. He is currently working as a freelance Lead Internal Quality Assurer in some colleges and training centres in London and delivers training on classroom control, management and strategies to some Private schools in Ghana.

Paapa has studied in four reputable universities in London to Doctoral level and is a speaker at universities, colleges, churches, and schools on 'Teaching in Prison as an Alternative Experience' and 'Reducing Reoffending'. He has mentored numerous assessors, teachers, tutors, lecturers, and internal verifiers/moderators in London. He is a dynamic and inspirational speaker and trainer on Internal

Quality Assurance (IQA) and Offender Education in England. He organises and delivers training workshops to IQA, Curriculum Managers, and Offender Education Managers in England. His training sessions are always oversubscribed.

Paapa Owusu-Manu is the Senior Pastor of Decision Time Church.

He is the founder of Decision Time Centre which deals with —

- Publication of Children's Educational Materials and resources.
- Children and Youth Mentoring (Decision Time Prison Talk).
- Offender and Ex-offender Education: Reducing crime and reoffending through biblical principles (Crime to Entrepreneurship).

Paapa has a passion to support orphans. Ten per cent of Decision Time Series proceeds are donated to orphans' education and their general well-being.

Enquiries & Contact: info@decisiontime.org.uk | www.decisiontime.org.uk

www.ingramcontent.com/pod-product-compliance
Lightning Source LLC
LaVergne TN
LVHW092102060526
838201LV00047B/1530